SEBASTIAN
[Super Sleuth]
and the
Crummy Yummies Caper

Mary Blount Christian

SEBASTIAN
[Super Sleuth]
and the
Crummy Yummies Caper

Illustrated by LISA McCUE

HARCOURT BRACE & COMPANY
Orlando Atlanta Austin Boston San Francisco Chicago Dallas New York
Toronto London

This edition is published by special
arrangement with Macmillan Publishing
Company, a division of Macmillan, Inc.

Grateful acknowledgment is made to
Macmillan Publishing Company, a division
of Macmillan, Inc. for permission to reprint
*Sebastian [Super Sleuth] and the Crummy
Yummies Caper* by Mary Blount Christian,
illustrated by Lisa McCue. Text copyright
© 1983 by Mary Blount Christian;
illustrations copyright © 1983 by Macmillan
Publishing Company.

Printed in the United States of America

ISBN 0-15-302174-8

2 3 4 5 6 7 8 9 10   035   97 96 95 94 93

For Julie and Finnegan

Contents

1

Shot!

Sebastian groaned and braced all four paws against the doorjamb of John's small car. He strained against the leash as his master tugged.

He knew John would eventually get him into the veterinarian's clinic. But there was no need to make it easy for him.

"Come on, big fella," John Quincy Jones coaxed. "You need your rabies shot." He sniffed, wrinkling his nose. "And a bath, too. You're a big doggie now, so quit acting like such a baby!"

Bath? Shot? It was even worse than Sebastian had first imagined. He whimpered miserably and cringed deeper into the worn car seat.

John disappeared from sight and Sebastian breathed a deep sigh of relief. But suddenly the door behind him opened and in one sneaky swoop John shoved against Sebastian's rump and sent him tumbling nose first to the ground.

"This is a fine way for a grown dog to act!" John scolded him as he lifted the wiggling Sebastian, opened the heavy oak door and shoved him into the doctor's waiting room.

Sebastian trembled and bellied over to one of the straight-backed metal chairs lining the walls and hid his head.

John sighed. "This hurts me as much as it does you. But you have to have your shots. And I can't let you go with me when you smell like a stinkweed, can I?"

Sebastian echoed John's sigh. He sniffed his own fur. He did smell a bit rank—could it have been the

onions in that hamburger, or perhaps the blue cheese in the dip last night?

John was right, of course. If he was going with John he had to smell better. And he *had* to go with John and that was that. He, Sebastian (Super Sleuth), was the greatest detective on four legs. His master, Detective John Quincy Jones of the City Police Department, couldn't solve a case without his expert help.

A master of disguises, Sebastian had a nose for clues. He had broken even the most difficult cases for CPD, although he never got any personal credit from that feline-loving chief of police! And not much from John, for that matter.

Still, that was no reason for him to behave like a puppy. Sebastian blushed beneath his fur. He slunk hangdog into a corner of the waiting room, leaving a wad of discarded fur on the floor.

The door to the examination room was flung open and Dr. Elizabeth Wright wiggled a finger at them. "Come on in," she said.

Sebastian wrinkled his nose at the smell of antiseptic cleaner that clung to the room. He and John groaned as his master lifted him onto the examination table.

The doctor slapped Sebastian's flank, then felt his furry tummy. "He's still overweight," she reminded John. "You really should feed him only Chummy Yummies until he's his proper weight, you know."

Sebastian curled his lip in disgust. Chummy Yummies, indeed! Bluch! They should be called Crummy Yummies! Besides, he was not too fat for his height—he was only a little short for his weight!

He trembled when he saw Dr. Wright hold up the vaccination needle. It seemed to get bigger every year.

She pushed the plunger slightly, sending a fine line of liquid into the air, then turned toward Sebastian.

He squeezed his eyes shut and yelped as the needle pierced his skin.

"Big baby!" she teased. "That didn't hurt a bit!"

Didn't hurt her, maybe! Sebastian thought angrily. He curled his lip at her.

"He needs a bath, too," John told Dr. Wright.

She wrinkled her nose slightly. "That he does! Do you want him to be show-ready, too?"

"Show-ready?" John asked.

"The All-Breed Dog Show, of course," Dr. Wright said. "We have a back room full of dogs being groomed for the show. It starts tomorrow." She felt Sebastian's tummy again. "Of course, he's not what you'd call a prime example of his breed—whatever that is. And he's not really in show shape. . . ."

John frowned, echoing Sebastian's own feelings about her reference to his savage good looks. "I just want him to smell better and look nice," John said. "I have to work tomorrow anyway and couldn't possibly enter him in a show."

Sebastian breathed a sigh of relief. Beauty contests! If only those judges knew the true qualities to look for—clever deduction, expertise at disguises, the ability to sniff out clue after hidden clue. He, Sebastian (Super Sleuth), wanted to be known as more than just another pretty dog face.

"Pick him up at four," Dr. Wright said, turning to ring for her assistant, Grimes.

Grimes came in and led Sebastian into a room with tubs and water hoses. There was an odor like flea dip and sweet-smelling powders all mixed together.

Grimes shoved the protesting Sebastian into one of the tubs and hosed him down. Sebastian had to admit the water felt soothing. But then Grimes lathered him with some icky-smelling suds. Sebastian sneezed, sending a thin layer of suds all over the aide.

It smelled like lady-dog suds, Sebastian thought. How humiliating!

As the assistant rubbed the lather into his fur Sebastian thumped his back foot rhythmically, splat, splat, splat. All the itchy places felt cool and nice. Then Grimes hosed off the lather.

Before Grimes had a chance to rub him down, Sebastian shook vigorously, slopping water onto both of them and all over the pale green walls. He curled his lip in satisfaction at a job well done as Grimes grumbled and toweled them both off.

The assistant then led Sebastian into a room filled with heat lamps and blow dryers. There he

brushed and blew until Sebastian's fur was dry and fluffy.

To add to Sebastian's humiliation, Grimes tied a big red bow around his neck and sprayed him with a doggie after-bath cologne called "Kennel Kapers."

Aaaaah-*chooo*! Sebastian sneezed repeatedly. Hooey! he thought. Now he smelled worse than ever.

He sulked in a dog run until John picked him up at four—not a moment too soon! Outside the clinic he spotted a freshly dug flower bed. Tugging with all his might Sebastian managed to pull himself over to it. He flipped to his back and rolled in the cool moist earth.

"Sebastian!" John scolded him. "I blew a whole day's pay on your grooming, and now you smell like fertilizer!"

Sebastian gave John a quick lick on the hand—one of those doggie tricks his mother had taught him. It always seemed to melt John's anger. Then he trotted toward the car, shaking off the excess dirt as he went.

John stopped off at the House o' Burgers and bought himself a cheeseburger and some fries. "I'm sorry, boy," he apologized to Sebastian. "But you can't have any. Dr. Wright says you're too fat. I'll give you some Chummy Yummies when we get home."

Sebastian sulked until John got stuck in a traffic jam. Then while John concentrated on not getting his car wrecked, Sebastian ate the burger and fries, sack and all.

"On top of everything, old boy, now you have onion breath!" John scolded as he let Sebastian into the apartment. "What am I going to do with you, you lovable old klutz?"

Sebastian was about to go into his humble, sorry dog routine when the phone rang, fortunately saving him from that embarrassing act.

"Trouble at the dog show, Chief?" John asked. "But what kind of trouble? Yes, I can check that out, sir."

Sebastian couldn't hear what the chief was saying. But his mind spun dizzily. It sounded like a new case. He'd have to help, of course. But what masterly disguise could he use at a dog show? Could he pose as a show judge, perhaps?

"Of course I'll take Sebastian along," John said. "It might even be fun for both of us."

Sebastian's mind whirled. The chief had actually suggested John take him along! At last, recognition for his true worth! It must be a really difficult case. Should he disguise himself as a vendor, perhaps?

He'd been with John to the rodeo once and the arena had stalls selling drinks and food and souvenirs. Surely a worthy event like a dog show would have the same.

"I'll register Sebastian in the show first thing in the morning, Chief," John said. He laughed. "Who knows? We might even win." He paused, frowning at the phone. "Well, you don't have to get insulting, Chief."

Sebastian's ears perked up. Enter? Of course. The perfect disguise! No one would suspect a thing. He'd go as an *ordinary dog*!

2

The Show-Offs

The next morning John and Sebastian stopped by the police station to see the chief.

Chief scowled at Sebastian from beneath his heavy eyebrows. "Are you sure that mutt of yours will pass as a real entry in the dog show? After all, people usually enter only the best."

Sebastian glared back at Chief. The only thing the two of them had in common was their love of Danish pastry. Chief's half-eaten roll sat on his desk, temptingly close to Sebastian's nose at that very moment.

"You mentioned trouble on the phone yesterday," John reminded Chief. "What kind of trouble are you expecting?"

Chief pulled a photograph from a folder marked *Operation Chummy*. He shoved it toward John. Sebastian strained to get a good look, too.

"As you may already know, Chummy the Wonder Dog will make a personal appearance at the show. She's the one that does all those Chummy Yummies commercials on television."

The photograph showed a St. Bernard standing on a cliff and looking out over a pasture below. It was the picture used on the box for those horrible-tasting pebbles they called Chummy Yummies, Sebastian noted.

He wrinkled his nose in disgust. Photographs could be retouched. All the movie stars had their photographs touched up to make them look younger and prettier. She was probably a lot fatter than the picture showed.

"Okay, Chief," John said. He scratched his chin in deep thought. "But what has the appearance of Chummy the Wonder Dog got to do with trouble at the All-Breed Dog Show?"

"In the last city where she appeared there was an attempt to kidnap her and hold her for ransom," Chief said. "She's insured for half a million dollars."

Humph! Sebastian thought, overpriced. No dog was worth that, except in rare cases, of course, where the dog was multitalented—like himself, Sebastian, the dread of all criminals. The commercials showed her swimming rivers to save drowning victims, and shooing little puppies out of the way of

11

speeding cars, and leaping from burning buildings to bring a little girl's favorite doll to her. Bunk!

Everybody knows all that Hollywood stuff is fake, Sebastian consoled himself. But had she ever solved a *real* mystery? No, he answered his own question. Not unless someone wrote it into a script for her. Chummy the Wonder Dog, indeed. The wonder is in what they see in her. Humph!

"I spoke to Chummy's manager on the phone," Chief said. "He didn't think much of our keeping a lookout on the dog's behalf—said he never let Chummy the Wonder Dog out of his sight."

"Oh?" John said. "He wasn't the one asking for help?"

"No," Chief replied. "We got a telephone call from the dog show director. You can talk with the manager when you get there. He'll be at the dog show with her today. You get down there with this walking fleatrap and see what you can do to make him look like a real show dog," Chief snapped.

Sebastian eased closer to Chief's Danish roll. The temptation was just too great. He snapped at it, swallowing it in one gulp.

"And get that hairy garbage-disposal out of here before I have him arrested for theft!" Chief yelled.

Outside, John tried to fluff Sebastian's fur. He put him on a leash. Sebastian trotted along, growling under his breath at the indignity of it all. He had managed so far to get through life without being led around like an ordinary house dog. Why did John have to start humiliating him now?

When they got to the arena where the dog show was, John commanded Sebastian to heel.

Sebastian trotted alongside John, consoling himself that a docile dog was as good a disguise as any. And if someone did try to kidnap that Hollywood beast, he, Sebastian (Super Sleuth), would catch the culprit. Then it would be *his* picture on the front pages of the newspapers, not that weird-looking St. Bernard's.

John stopped at the registration desk and asked for an entry blank. The woman glanced at Sebastian and raised an eyebrow.

"This is the dog you're entering?" she asked. A slight smile played across her lips.

Sebastian fought the urge to snap at her fat ankles.

"When we say All-Breed Dog Show we don't mean all breeds in one dog," she said.

John raised his eyebrow right back at her. "I'll have you know he's a purebred. I have his papers, I assure you."

"I'd guess his only papers are spread over the kitchen floor! But fill this in," she said, her nose in

13

the air. "And find someplace to groom him until your category is called."

She snickered, then turned to repeat her instructions to the next people. Sebastian and John made their way through the scattered cages and portable grooming tables.

A terrier stood statue-still while a woman in a white jacket brushed and fluffed and sprayed his fur.

Ahhhh-*chooo*! Sebastian sneezed. He was certainly glad that John hadn't tried to make *him* smell like a petunia!

At one cage a man sprinkled baby powder into the white collar of a collie. "It'll make the white look even whiter," the man told John.

Farther down a woman used a charcoal stick to black out a tiny white spot on the neck of her nearly all-black cocker spaniel.

Humph! Sebastian thought, cosmetics! What kind of show was this, anyway? Whatever happened to natural beauty, like his, for instance? That rugged, macho look without paints and powders?

"Well, hello there!" a woman's voice called. "I thought you had to work today."

It was Dr. Wright. She clutched a chihuahua in her arms. That figures, Sebastian thought. No wonder she's always saying he's overweight. She's

used to looking at that mouse masquerading as a dog.

"Why, er, ah . . . ." John mumbled. He seemed stumped for a ready answer.

Sebastian moaned. John was never too swift with the cover stories. Realizing right then and there that it was up to him, Sebastian leaped up, placing his paws on Dr. Wright's shoulders so she could get a good look at the entry tag on his collar. The chihuahua yipped and snapped at him.

Dr. Wright stroked her dog soothingly. "Oh, I see you've entered Sebastian in the show after all. Not in the obedience trials, I hope." She shoved him down and burst into a fit of giggles.

"Heel, boy," John said, blushing. "I—I was able to get the day off after all," he told her.

Sebastian breathed a sigh of relief. It sure took John long enough to think of an answer!

"Have you seen anything—er—unusual here?" John asked her.

"The most unusual thing around here is Sebastian," she replied, punctuating it with another rude snicker.

Sebastian stared at her leg, imagining how he'd enjoy taking a nip out of it about then.

"They're expecting Chummy the Wonder Dog to arrive any minute," she said. "And as the official

16

vet for the show I'd better make my rounds and see that there're no problems." She nodded good-by.

Chummy, Chummy, Chummy! Sebastian thought to himself. So what was the big deal? Just an empty-headed Hollywood dog, if you asked him. Chummy, indeed! Dummy, more like it.

Suddenly a nervous man with glasses and a dark handlebar moustache sprang toward John through the crowd. "Are you that detective I'm supposed to meet?" he asked.

"Why—er—yes," John muttered. "But I'm supposed to be undercover. How did you know?"

"I'm Chummy the Wonder Dog's manager. Your chief said to look for a man with a funny-looking, overweight dog that smelled like fertilizer."

Sebastian curled his lip.

"Hmm, well, yes?" John replied, blushing.

The manager held a paper out to John. "This was shoved under the door to Chummy's dressing room," the manager said.

Sebastian raised himself up on his hind legs so he could see, too. Letters had been cut from magazines and newspapers to form the message:

BEWARE! THE DOG SHOW COULD BE A REAL BOMB!

It was signed, THE DOG CATCHER.

3
So, Where's the Bomb?

Bomb! The word hung in the air around them like a dark cloud. Sebastian could feel his fur prickle along his spine. He knew from the pale look on John's face that he, too, was scared.

"We've got to empty the building," John told Chummy's manager. "We'll get everyone out. Then Sebastian and I will try to find the bomb."

Sebastian whimpered. Sebastian and I, he thought. Why Sebastian? Why me? Why should I have to stay here and look for the bomb? Get the bomb squad, he thought frantically, the bomb squad! Oh, if only John could understand him.

"I'll call the bomb squad at once," John said at last.

Sebastian breathed a sigh of relief.

"Meanwhile," John said to the director of the dog show, "you pretend there's a fire drill. Tell the people this is a new fire code, a rule for large gatherings like this. But get them all outside without any panic. Sebastian and I will look for the bomb until the experts get here. Maybe we'll have it located by then. And as soon as you get everyone out, go stay with Chummy the Wonder Dog and her manager. Make sure she doesn't get near here."

Sebastian sighed wearily. His heart did a flip-flop. His mother always told him to be brave, even when he was scared. Oh, if only he had nine lives like a stupid cat!

Over the loudspeaker system the show's director announced the fire drill. "It's only a drill, folks," he told them. His huge round glasses slipped down his nose as he spoke. He shoved them back with a trembling hand and continued. "There's no reason for panic."

No reason for panic? Sebastian thought grimly. Maybe no reason for the show director to panic. He gets to go outside with the others.

John came back from telephoning the bomb squad. "Okay, big fellow," he said, patting Sebastian on the head. "It's up to you and me."

The nasty lady from the registration desk hurried by carrying a strongbox. Sebastian figured that was the money she'd collected from the entrants. If the bomb scare was a trick to empty the building and

get to the money at least that wouldn't work, he consoled himself.

John pulled out one of his bullets and popped it open. He shoved some of the gunpowder under Sebastian's nose. "Smell this, boy. See if you can find a package that smells something like this."

Sebastian sneezed. The gunpowder spread over John's dark trousers.

"Let's go, boy. Sniff!" John commanded. He dropped to his knees and peeked under the ruffle that surrounded the registration desk.

Sebastian trotted to the spectator benches. To his delight he found that many of the people had gone outside so quickly they'd left behind half-eaten hotdogs, hamburgers and assorted snacks.

Methodically Sebastian ate them up as he made his way along the benches. And what better way to find the bomb than to get rid of everything else? Someone could have hidden it under one of those delicious appetizers.

The sound of sirens grew nearer, then stopped just outside. The bomb squad arrived. Within minutes four men in protective flak suits brought in two police dogs and unleashed them.

"Find!" one of the uniformed men commanded. The dogs rushed past Sebastian, their noses pushed to the floor, sniffling loudly.

Sebastian quickly gobbled down a pair of hamburgers. He saw no reason to let those beasts with their vacuum cleaner noses get to the food.

Fortunately, the dogs must have been trained to wait for their rewards until after their missions. They returned to their masters later and were re-leashed.

"Nothing," the bomb squad captain told John. "Let me see that threatening note again."

"Going to be a real bomb," John read aloud. "It doesn't exactly sound like there's a bomb here, does it?" he asked. "It sounds almost like a newspaper review of a bad play, now that I reread it." John

scratched his chin in thought. "It seems more like a threat to ruin the dog show somehow. But how?"

Sebastian licked the last of the mustard and catsup from his whiskers and trotted closer to John. He felt as content as a full tick and relieved that there was no real bomb.

He sank to the floor next to John's feet to think. What had the criminal accomplished by this, if it were a threat and not a real bomb? Maybe he only wanted to scare people so they'd go home. Then the show would turn out to be a real bomb, just like the note threatened.

But somehow he didn't think that was the whole plan. What if having everyone outside the building were only *part* of his plan? What if they had done exactly what he wanted them to do by leaving?

He glanced toward the table where the gold-plated trophies had been. They were still there. There hadn't been a robbery during the "fire drill."

John turned the note over and over in his hands. "I just don't feel that the danger is over," he told the bomb squad captain. "All that has happened so far has only delayed the show. But I feel like this must have something to do with that dog star, Chummy the Wonder Dog."

Maybe the manager made all this up just for the publicity, Sebastian thought. He'd heard about those eccentric stars that did silly things, even claimed phony kidnappings, just to get publicity.

The bomb squad left. The people with their dogs came back inside. Soon the building was jammed again. Sebastian glanced around him. Maybe the criminal was right there in front of his very eyes. Was he one of the spectators? That man with the cane, maybe? Or one of the people with a show dog? Any one of those people showing off their dogs might be guilty.

Perhaps someone wanted to scare off most of the dogs, cut down on the competition.

Or maybe someone wanted to call more attention to the dog show. Nothing like a good bomb scare to get all the news reporters and cameras to cover an otherwise rather dull event.

Of course, that motive made him suspicious of the show director, too. The more publicity, the more money the show would bring in. And who might profit from that? The director? Or, might Chummy the Wonder Dog get part of the profits for her appearance? Her owners would get most of that. Of course, they were the ones that asked Chief to help. But wouldn't her manager get part of it too?

Or maybe it was not a man at all. Maybe it was a woman—he shouldn't be so chauvinistic, he scolded himself.

"The show schedule has been changed," John said aloud. "Your show judging won't be for another hour. And I guess the special appearance of Chummy the Wonder Dog won't be until later this afternoon now."

Sebastian yawned. He could wait.

"Let's go take a look at Chummy the Wonder Dog, old fellow," John told Sebastian. "Let's just see for ourselves what all the rave reviews are about, shall we?"

Sebastian trotted alongside his master, his own thoughts racing through the sparse clues. Who made the threat? Was it a real threat? Or was it only someone's idea of a practical joke?

Was it a means to get to the money the show would bring in? The trophies? Those awards were gold and silver, after all. Or was John right? Did everything point to Chummy the Wonder Dog?

If John had ruined the criminal's plans, would he try something else now? Something worse, maybe?

4
In the Doghouse

Chummy's dressing room was a large air-conditioned mobile home with her name scrolled across the sides. Wow! Sebastian thought enviously, that is *some* doghouse.

Parked in the shadow of the arena building, it was surrounded by a ring of security officers in blue uniforms. They were hired by the show director to keep the curious crowds and pawprint seekers from getting too close.

"Hold it!" one of the men called out to John as he and Sebastian approached them.

John flashed his badge as identification. "Detective John Quincy Jones, CPD," he said.

The man looked at Sebastian.

"He's with me," John explained.

The officer hid a half-eaten doughnut behind his back. "I don't think he ought to go inside," he said, nodding toward Sebastian. "He might give fleas to the star."

Sebastian curled his lip indignantly.

John raised an eyebrow. "He's just been bathed, I'll have you know!" he protested.

The guard let them pass with a shrug.

As they passed Sebastian managed to filch the rest of the doughnut from the guard's grasp. He swallowed it whole, belching contentedly. Fleas, indeed, he thought haughtily.

A man opened the door to John's knock. He motioned for them to come in. He introduced himself as Jimmy Jamm, publicity director for Chummy Yummies. Mr. Jamm had a tie clasp in the shape of a dog bone and a smile like an alligator's.

The manager's voice carried loudly from the next room. It sounded as if he were on the phone with someone. "I'm doing my best! It's not my fault! She insists on keeping the air conditioning so cold in here. She's behaving like a spoiled—yessir. Yessir. I understand. Of course, I love my job. Thank you, sir. Yes, I'll take care of her. Good-by."

There was a loud clack as the receiver was slammed into its cradle. The manager came out. His moustache drooped in surprise at seeing John and Sebastian there. "Oh, dear," he apologized. "The star's 'parents' were just a little concerned for her— no problem, heh, heh."

While John shook hands Sebastian stared at the dark wood-grained walls. They were practically covered with glossy photos of Chummy the Wonder Dog—Chummy to the rescue, Chummy on a bearskin rug, Chummy on the Johnny Carson show, Chummy, Chummy and more Chummy. Totally tasteless, Sebastian thought—as tasteless as Chummy Yummies.

The star herself lounged on a canopied doggie bed. A faint snore drifted from beneath the ruffled cover.

"She got a sore throat," the manager said. "She can't bark a word and the doctor thought she should get some rest before her appearance. Besides, she needs a little beauty nap before appearing in public," he said with a nervous wink.

It'll take more than a nap to make that fleatrap a beauty, Sebastian thought in disgust. He was willing to bet two steak bones that her fur was retouched. Humph!

While he stared, Chummy the Wonder Dog stretched and yawned, then stared at them blankly.

Can't even nod a hello without a script, Sebastian fumed. And he was pretty sure he spotted a gold cap on one of her teeth when she yawned. He glanced around the room.

There were framed keys to cities that various mayors had presented to her, a gold statue for acting, although he couldn't understand how she got that, and a door, opening to a small closet. Inside were hair suits! Sebastian couldn't believe it! There were at least three changes of fur, all exactly alike, hanging in the closet. So she wouldn't get burrs caught in her *real* fur in those dangerous scenes, he guessed. Or maybe they were for her to wear when she was shedding.

And on every table were bowls of Chummy Yummies—cheese-flavored, beef-flavored and egg-flavored Chummy Yummies. Yech!

John slid into one of the red leather chairs across from the manager. "I have reason to believe that the bomb threat was only meant to throw us off guard," he told the man.

The manager stroked his moustache with one finger and shifted in his chair. "From what?" he asked.

John shrugged slightly. "Well, Chummy the Wonder Dog has nearly been kidnapped before. And that note was delivered right to you, not to the director of the show. I think this is meant to distract us from Chummy. Maybe there'll be another attempt made to kidnap her."

The manager waved his arms in a wide circle. "As you saw outside, there're more guards here than the president has. Kidnapping her would be impossible. I was doing all right with her. But now her owners sent their own security. I don't know why the show director brought in the police on this. You aren't really needed, I assure you."

Sebastian's ears perked up. So it was the owners of the dog and not Chummy's manager who hired the security guards. Interesting. Very interesting.

"Perhaps you're right," John said. "Maybe I'll just hang around and let my dog participate in the show and just forget all this silly business."

Sebastian couldn't believe his fuzzy ears. John giving up? Just as things got interesting? No way!

He, Sebastian (Super Sleuth), was sure something extraordinary was about to happen. And *he* was not about to give up on it, even if it meant going through that humiliating beauty pageant.

Chummy the Wonder Dog yawned and stretched (yes, her teeth were definitely capped, Sebastian noted). She sat and offered her paw to John.

"Smart dog!" John said admiringly.

Sebastian turned on his heels. Show-off! he thought. Who *couldn't* shake hands—when he really wanted to, that is? When the manager opened the door for them, Jimmy Jamm reached into his pocket and pulled out a delicious-looking bone. "For your doggie," he said, jamming the bone into Sebastian's willing mouth.

Yech! Chummy Yummies must be making artificial bones now, too! Ptuiiiy! Sebastian spat it out.

"Come on, big fellow," John called to Sebastian. "I've got to comb and groom you. It is a perfect excuse to hang around and keep my eyes open for trouble."

Sebastian breathed a sigh of relief. Good! he thought. For a moment he'd been afraid all that training he'd given John in police work had been for nothing. But John was suspicious, too.

On the way from the mobile dressing room John and Sebastian were stopped by the security guards again.

Curious, Sebastian thought. Those guards were so doggone careful about who went in and out of Chummy's trailer and what they had with them. Yet that manager said the note was shoved under the dressing room door. How?

Sebastian broke loose and trotted toward the garbage can at the rear of the trailer. You can tell a lot about people by the garbage they throw out, he knew. He hoped to see evidence that Chummy didn't eat Chummy Yummies at all. What a sensation that'd make! He poked his nose in.

There were some magazines and old newspapers. They were shredded as if someone had cut letters from them.

"Sebastian," John snapped at him. He grabbed the leash that dangled from Sebastian's neck. "Shame! You mustn't raid garbage cans. Be a proud doggie! If you're hungry, I'll get you something to eat. I understand they have complimentary Chummy Yummies in the main building."

Tug as he might, Sebastian couldn't get John back to look in the garbage can. A perfectly good clue and he couldn't make the one human who needed it see it.

It looked as if once again it was up to him, Sebastian (Super Sleuth), to solve the mystery.

He sighed. Humans could be so difficult to help sometimes.

5

Catastrophe!

John ran the brush through Sebastian's fur, tugging at the small tangles, but keeping one eye on the crowd as it milled through the grooming areas around the show ring. Sebastian's back foot thumped in rhythm with the brush, but his keen mind was sorting through the clues he'd uncovered so far.

The problem with that good clue he'd found in the garbage behind Chummy's trailer, Sebastian figured, was that it still didn't narrow down the suspects very much.

At least four guards surrounded the trailer at all times. Yet, any one of them could have let someone in to deliver that note. Or even planted it there himself. And of course the manager or even Chummy could have put it there.

He ruled out Chummy. Although she could maybe paste the note together (with stage direction), he doubted that she knew how to spell well enough.

Still, she might be greedy enough for publicity to try anything. So, he decided, he should probably keep her on his list of suspects.

Plenty of other people could go in and out without the guards thinking much about it. The director of the show or delivery people, maybe even television or newspaper reporters. That publicity-happy Chummy would let any one of them in.

"Come on, big fellow," John urged, interrupting his thoughts. "They're calling your class in judging. We have to make this look good," he said, patting Sebastian on the head.

John led Sebastian into the ring. Sebastian eased into a sitting position, glancing around him at the competition. Not much of it, he concluded.

"Up!" John commanded in a tone Sebastian thought was unnecessarily sharp. "The judge is watching you!"

Sebastian yipped as he was rudely jerked to his feet. He trotted at John's heels in a circle with the other dogs. Let the rest of the pack think he was just an ordinary dog, he thought icily.

"Reverse your dogs," the judge ordered.

Sebastian's toenails clicked against the wooden floor as he turned sharply in the opposite direction. Good military about-face, he congratulated himself. Let the judge make a note of that!

A wave of excited murmurs swept through the crowd. Sebastian was sure it was in admiration of his sharp-order drill. Or—horror of horrors!—had they seen through his clever disguise as an ordinary dog? It was so difficult to hide one's true talent. But no, the people were looking in another direction.

Cameras flashed. Applause rippled through the arena. Chummy the Wonder Dog was making her grand entrance into the building.

Wouldn't you know she'd come just in time to interrupt his performance? he thought bitterly. Probably on purpose.

"Heel," John commanded. Sebastian slowed to a walk, feeling his fur brush John's leg.

"Stand firm," the judge commanded.

The people brought their dogs to a halt. The judge stopped in front of each of them, examining the entry's eyes, teeth, posture and so on.

The judge stopped in front of Sebastian, who sucked in his breath as the judge poked at his rib cage.

"Overweight," the judge said. "Smells a bit like garden fertilizer, too. Didn't you prepare for this show?"

He pulled down Sebastian's lip. "Has he been eating onions?" the judge asked.

Sebastian reached out his pink tongue and gave

the judge a quick wet slurp across the nose. The man may be rude, but he was the judge after all. One must respect power.

"Blech!" the judge yelled. "Your dog doesn't know the first thing about being a show dog!"

John blushed, chuckling. "I hope you won't take this as attempted bribery."

"Humph," the judge mumbled, moving to the next entry.

The judge finally went back to the center and called for his assistant to bring the ribbons. He held the third-place yellow ribbon in his hand. Sebastian wiggled in eager anticipation.

"Third place goes to Roughcut Gem," he called out.

As the owner led his dog to the center to collect the ribbon Sebastian sighed. Of course—definitely an inferior dog, he thought, pitying the poor beast. So the judge had decided to heighten the suspense by saving the best for last. So be it. He was ready whenever called.

"Second place goes to Familiar Face," the judge announced. He handed the red ribbon to the dog's owner.

Not bad, Sebastian thought, but still not close to his own macho beauty.

"First pl—" the judge began.

Sebastian twitched excitedly, ready to spring to the center and get his first-place blue ribbon. But the judge's words faded and his face paled. He stared open-mouthed somewhere beyond Sebastian and John.

Before Sebastian could turn to see what the judge was looking at, a cat the color of raw pumpkin sprang into the winner's circle, hissing and puffing her fur until she looked like a plump balloon.

"Meeeee-*ow*!" she screamed.

A low howl grew into yelping, barking, growling and a scramble of legs and leashes as every dog in the arena with the exception, of course, of him, Sebastian (Super Sleuth), moved toward the lone feline.

She leap-frogged across their backs, screeching like a banshee, and frantically grabbed at one of the stage curtains at one end of the arena, clutching it with her sharp claws.

Nearly every dog in the building dragged a protesting handler to the curtain and leaped, snarled and snapped at the cat, whose fur stood on end. Her eyes blazed and she screamed once more.

"Ladies and gentlemen, *please*!" the show director begged. He shoved his owllike glasses back onto his nose. "Heel your dogs. You *must* heel your dogs!"

Sebastian yawned and settled into a heap on the floor to watch the commotion. He was not about to get his paws trampled on in a free-for-all over one ill-tempered cat.

John patted him. "Good boy," he bragged. "They don't see *you* running after that poor cat, disrupting the show. I just hope the judge is watching you now."

Gradually the people got their dogs under control. A man in a white jump suit brought a ladder and a small carrier cage. He climbed to the top and finally pulled the frightened cat (and part of the curtain) into the cage.

Howls of protest still punctuated the air in the arena. Gradually things settled to just a few noisy protests.

"How on earth did a cat get in here?" John wondered aloud to no one in particular.

Indeed, Sebastian thought, how? He figured the cat didn't voluntarily march into a building full of her archenemies. Someone must have deliberately forced her inside. But why?

Was it to cause one more disruption of the show —one more delay? And for what purpose?

The answer came all too quickly. Chummy's manager rushed up to John. Perspiration dotted his pale face and clung to his moustache. He swept his stained sleeve across his face, leaving a small smudge of brown on his cheek.

"You were supposed to stop it! And what are you doing? What am I to do? What am I going to tell all these people who expect to see Chummy the Wonder Dog perform? What I am going to tell her owners?"

"Calm down," John said, "and tell me what you're talking about."

"Chummy!" the manager yelled, making his moustache wiggle on his lip. "She's been dognapped from right under your very nose!"

6

New Dog in Town

"Lock all the doors!" John shouted. "Don't let any-one leave this arena!"

The show director paled when he heard the news about Chummy. His glasses slipped right down to the tip of his nose. But he announced that everyone must stay right where he was. "Do not leave until you are dismissed by this gentleman here," he said, pointing to Detective John Quincy Jones.

The guards quickly snapped the doors shut.

John rushed to telephone Chief. Sebastian could hear Chief's angry shouting even though he was not that close to the telephone.

"But it could happen to anyone," John protested. "Yes, Chief. Yes, of course. I understand. The water-front beat, you say? No, Chief. I wouldn't like that assignment. I'll find Chummy the Wonder Dog right away, Chief."

41

He hung up the phone. "Oh, Sebastian," John said. "If only I could make you understand. We must find Chummy the Wonder Dog. I just wish there were some way *you* could help me."

Sebastian licked John's hand. Why was it so hard for his master to understand? Hadn't he, Sebastian (Super Sleuth), solved every single case John had ever worked on?

Even with a cold he could sniff out clues better than any other detective in the world. But John just didn't realize that he, Sebastian (Super Sleuth), understood the language, even if he didn't speak it fluently.

So how much canine language did John speak? It made their relationship so difficult at times. Sebastian sighed. No matter, he'd do his best with or without John's understanding. He'd find that stupid movie star and save John's job for him.

Sebastian trotted toward the stage. Those curtains would be a good place to hide a dog, especially one with a sore throat who couldn't make a sound in her own behalf. He bent down to peek under the curtain. Nothing there but dust. Ah-*choo*!

John had reacted pretty quickly in shutting off the escape routes. Maybe the kidnapper and Chummy the Wonder Dog were still in the building somewhere. Sebastian decided to check the bleachers.

42

Sebastian crawled over and under the bleacher stands. Only a few scraps from hot dogs and hamburgers there. He snapped them up hurriedly.

He dashed behind the stands, peering into the dark corners. He saw the show director bending over an overweight blob of mahogany fur, peering through his owllike glasses at something. Was it Chummy the Wonder Dog? The director was looking at the dog's tag. Was he trying to switch tags? Make the old Super Sleuth think this was another dog?

The dog yawned and blinked sleepily at him. Same empty eyes, Sebastian observed. But the teeth hadn't been capped. Definitely not Chummy the Wonder Dog. The director seemed to be only checking the identity of the dog. Still, he'd bear watching, the cunning canine concluded. This didn't automatically eliminate him as a suspect.

He dogtrotted along the stalls, peering into each one. He saw the man with the cane brushing black dye onto his graying terrier. The man looked up at him, wiping a smudge of black across his nose as he did. Sebastian stuck his keen nose into the air and sniffed. The dye the man was applying to his dog smelled a lot like that polish John used on his shoes to make them shine. Wouldn't you think a dog could just grow old gracefully? he wondered, hurrying on.

Sebastian saw Labrador retrievers getting their nails clipped and chows being fluffed and dried. But no Chummy the Wonder Dog.

The cages lined up in the alley offered no clues, either. Undaunted, the cavalier canine loped toward the restrooms, the only place he hadn't checked.

Someone had thrown that pumpkin cat into the arena on purpose. Whoever had put that note under the dressing room door earlier probably did it. And whoever put the cat in the arena must have Chummy the Wonder Dog. But who?

He pushed through the swinging door and came face-to-face with the ugliest poodle he'd ever seen. It was grossly oversized and its pompoms were poorly trimmed and uneven. It even smelled funny —like shoe polish, maybe. And they talked about his onions! The ugly poodle was chained to a sink pipe. There was no one in the restroom but the two of them. Maybe someone had abandoned the poor ugly animal, hoping someone else would adopt it. What better place to find a foster parent than at a dog show?

The poodle looked at Sebastian with huge blank eyes. It opened its mouth to say something, but emitted only a faint squeak. A gold-capped tooth glittered.

Sebastian acknowledged the greeting politely,

then rummaged through the big wastebasket in the corner.

No Chummy the Wonder Dog there. Just a lot of white and mahogany colored hair clippings and an empty bottle of brown dye, probably cosmetic treatment for one of those beauty contestants out there.

Sebastian pushed out into the arena again, searching for some sign of Chummy the Wonder Dog. A St. Bernard is hard to hide, especially one that big and with a gold tooth and those stupid expressionless eyes—the Orphan Annie of the canine world.

Suddenly Sebastian stopped in his tracks. It

would be hard to hide a big, dopey St. Bernard, unless, of course, she was disguised as something else. Say a poodle? A huge ugly poodle? No wonder that dog looked so awful!

He raced back to the restroom. How clever of someone to disguise her as a different breed. No one would be looking for a poodle! He grabbed the leash between his teeth and worked it loose from the pipe. Slipping his paw into the loop, he led Chummy the Wonder Dog through the crowded arena.

He spotted John. Chief had arrived and was bawling John out. Sebastian trotted up to John and pushed against his hand with his cold nose.

"Stop, boy," John scolded. "Can't you see I have enough trouble?"

Sebastian pushed again.

Chief looked down. He burst into laughter. "I might have known that the only girlfriend that mutt of yours could get would be one just as ugly and stupid as he is."

John scowled at Chief's uncalled-for remark, then stooped to rub a brown smudge on his pants leg, muttering. He was eye-to-eye with Chummy the Wonder Dog. "I know those eyes from somewhere. But where?"

Frantically, Sebastian tried to think how he could give John a big hint. He barked his deep, throaty bark.

Chummy opened her mouth. She looked like she was barking, but she only squeaked like a mouse instead.

"Of course!" John said. "Chief, *this* is Chummy! I've found her. She's a little the worse for wear, but she is here."

He turned to Sebastian. "Good boy," he said. "You accidentally hung your foot on her leash and brought her to me."

Drat! Sebastian thought angrily. How could John be so *dense* as to think this is an accident?

John reached down to pet Chummy the Wonder Dog. "But we haven't caught her kidnapper. If we don't, he'll surely try again."

At least John was beginning to think as cleverly as he, Sebastian (Super Sleuth). They needed to catch the kidnapper. But there were so many suspects.

There was an arena full of exhibitors and their dogs who might want to see Chummy the Wonder Dog gone for one reason or another (money, or maybe the hope of having their dog take her place as the mascot of the Chummy Yummies products). Still, his keen instincts, proof he was the best four-legged detective in the world, told Sebastian that it was somebody close to the overrated canine star.

Was it the show director, hoping to gain a little national publicity for the All-Breed Dog Show here?

Or perhaps the owners, who would rather have the insurance money than that stupid dog? They might have cleverly called in the police to throw them off the track.

Was it Jimmy Jamm with his alligator smile and his yucky free dog bones? Maybe he wanted a new image for his company's product—something other than a lump of mahogany fur with empty eyes.

Or might it be the manager? He was disturbed that the show director had called in the police and that the owners had hired security guards to protect Chummy the Wonder Dog.

He stared at the brown stain on John's pants. He'd seen another like it—and recently. The man with the cane and the graying terrier? That was black. But it smudged the same. Suddenly he remembered. Chummy's manager had had a brown smear on his shirt sleeve when he came to tell John that Chummy the Wonder Dog was gone. And it was fresh, too. It'd left a smear on his face when he wiped his face with his sleeve.

And Sebastian was willing to bet a steak dinner that the brown smear on John matched the brown on Chummy and that bottle of dye in the restroom. In fact, if he could just get John to look in there, the bottle might even have fingerprints on it—the manager's.

How could he make John follow him to the clue? Sebastian suddenly jumped up and snatched John's notebook. He dashed toward the restroom.

"Wait!" John shouted. "Wait! Now what on earth has gotten into that silly dog? Come back, Sebastian!"

Sebastian pushed into the restroom. He waited until John could see him, then he dropped the notebook into the trashcan.

"Bad doggie!" John scolded him. "Shame!"

He reached into the trashcan to get his notebook. "Well, well! What have we here?" John asked. "Hmmm."

Carefully he slipped his pencil into the mouth of the bottle and lifted it from the trashcan. He slipped it into a plastic bag from his pocket.

"This looks like the same color dye as Chummy's hair," he said. "And all that hair in there is probably hers too.

"But who did this?" John asked.

Frantically Sebastian thought. How could he get John to see the manager's arm with the dye smear on it?

"Now, as for you—" John said, turning once more to scold Sebastian.

Sebastian turned on his heels and pushed through the door. He dashed across the arena as the manager walked toward Chief and Chummy the Wonder Dog.

"Wait, Sebastian!" John shouted. "Stop!"

But Sebastian didn't stop until he'd flung himself, dead dog style, in front of the manager. The manager tumbled headfirst over him, landing on all fours to come face-to-face with the super sleuth himself.

"I'm so sorry," John said, reaching to give the manager a hand. "I just don't know what has come over him. The excitement and—" John grabbed the manager's arm, the one with the smear.

"Here, now," John said. "What's this?"

7
Gratitude, Yech!

As fast as a foxhound, John slapped the handcuffs on Chummy's manager. Sebastian was gratified to see that Chief was completely surprised—almost as surprised as Chummy's manager! And Sebastian thought that Chief was maybe even a little impressed by their fast work in solving the case.

Two uniformed officers quickly took the manager off to jail. All the way out he was yelling that he was glad it was over. "At least I won't have to be around that dumb dog anymore! I'm tired of looking after her, of getting the blame when she gets sick. Is it my fault she wants the mobile dressing room so cold all the time? Dumb dog!"

The show director led Chummy the Wonder Dog back to her dressing room where they slipped her into one of her specially made fur coats. When she returned to the arena later for her second personal appearance she looked like she was expected to look —glamorous and composed.

To Sebastian's horror and embarrassment, Chummy the Wonder Dog marched right up and gratefully kissed him—a great big wet slurp on his blushing cheek! How humiliating! And to make it even worse a newspaper photographer snapped their picture at that magic moment and the next morning it was spread all over the papers.

John bought six papers. Two for himself and Sebastian, one to send to his mother, one for Chief, and two to send to the kennel where Sebastian was born.

Sebastian had to admit he looked terrific—the perfect image of a macho detective dog.

John stopped by Chief's office to give him his copy of the newspaper.

Chief grumbled appropriately, although Sebastian noted that he was hiding his own copy behind his back.

"As much as I hate to admit it, I guess we owe this case to Sebastian," Chief said, much to the super sleuth's surprise.

"If he hadn't accidentally caught Chummy's leash," Chief added, to Sebastian's consternation, "she might have been whisked away and her owners would've been forced to buy her back. The owners weren't too happy with the job Chummy's manager was doing. They'd threatened to fire him. I guess he wanted to be sure he had plenty of money, even if he didn't have a job."

"If Sebastian hadn't been in such a frisky mood, taking my notepad like that, I might never have discovered that empty bottle of dye, and broken the case," John added.

Sebastian scowled. They didn't give him any credit at all. They'd paid no attention to his terrific clue about the cut-up newspapers. If they had, they'd have known the manager was a suspect. And now that he thought about it, the manager probably lied about the note being slipped under the door. No wonder the guards didn't see anyone! He clipped Chummy poodle style and dyed her fur while everyone else was trying to capture that cat. He had to hurry—no wonder it was such a sloppy job. He probably planned to slip her out as soon as it was safe.

Next thing you knew, Chief and John would think catching the manager was their idea, too!

"And if Sebastian weren't so klutzy and hadn't run into the manager you might not have noticed that telltale smear of dye, either," Chief said.

Sebastian curled his lip. When would he ever be acknowledged as the great super sleuth he was?

"And what is that trophy you're holding out for me to notice and comment on?" Chief asked. "Don't tell me that mutt actually won Best of Show!"

John blushed. "Not exactly, Chief. He didn't get any of the beauty prizes. But he did win Mr. Congeniality! I think it might've been because he didn't chase the cat like all the others."

The Chief guffawed. "Laziness is more likely the reason than congeniality." Chief cleared his throat. "I've decided to reward Sebastian properly for his help, minor and accidental as it might have been."

"Gosh, Chief. That's really nice of you!" John said. "You hear that, boy? A reward!"

Sebastian perked up his ears and thumped his tail anxiously.

"Knowing that four-legged garbage-disposal, I'm sure he'd rather have a prize he can eat," Chief continued.

Something to eat? Sebastian's mind was dizzy with tasty images. Steak? Pizza? Maybe something really fancy, like pheasant under glass?

"I talked with Chummy's owner," Chief said. "And after I told him about Sebastian he was so grateful. He's giving Sebastian a lifetime supply of Chummy Yummies!"

Sebastian felt his stomach churn. Crummy Yummies? Bluch!

How could they be so inhuman? he asked himself as he trotted out to the car to wait for John. And after he'd solved their case for them—once again?

He sighed. At least he had the satisfaction of knowing that he'd done a good job, unheralded as he might be.

And he'd used the most masterful and difficult disguise in his entire career—that of an *ordinary dog*!